This book belongs to

Are we grateful enough?

Zabed Mohammad, PhD.
Educator & Researcher
Canada

Edited by
Robert Hart

Editorial Assistants
Fatema Yeasmin

Zarir Shiddike

Kids Edu Care

Hey, I know you are my good friend. Could you tell me... To whom should I be grateful? And why should I be grateful?
Certainly! It's an interesting question!

I am also thinking like you. Sometimes.... Well, most of the time. But it's difficult to think about!
What do you mean it's difficult?

Let's think about it together! What could have given us the ability to think about things that pop into our heads? How do we think?
Look! I know that I have a powerful brain, and I can think about what I like! So why should I be grateful? And to whom?

Well
Cows and goats also have brains...
But they cannot think the
way we humans think.
Yes, you are right.
I am not arguing with you.

Sure, let's think about that I also have a powerful brain, but if I am not healthy, can I think effectively?
But I am not talking about animals.

You know about people with brain disorders?
Have you seen them?
Are they able to think the way we do?
So, at this moment,
shouldn't we be grateful?
Well,
Grateful to whom?

Wait a minute! Think about our eyes! If dust or something gets into our eyes, doesn't it bother us? How uncomfortable we feel? Not only that, they help us see the beauty of our surroundings!
My eyes are okay, and I can see. I think that that's their job. I shouldn't be worried about that!

Wait! Think about our ears, and how they help us listen.
Oh... I am sorry. I know someone who cannot hear properly, and when they went to the doctor, the doctor said they could not identify the problem, and there was nothing they could do. That would be awful! So, for that, I suppose, I should be grateful that I still have my hearing!

Yes, that's what I mean. Also, think about our noses, how they help us to breathe and smell things.
Yeah! Last week my nose was very stuffed up. It was bothering me a lot!

Yeah, I heard about that, and it scares me.
During COVID-19,
too many people died like that.
I don't want to go back to those days!
Oh, yeah.
That happens to me a lot.
But at least we're not like people who need help breathing.

What?
What is COVID-19?
Oh, it was a pandemic that affected our entire world.
It started with people feeling like they just had a cold, but then it suddenly affected their breathing,
and many people died. What do you think? I'm certainly grateful that didn't happen to us!

Kids Edu Care School
80
COVID 19
STAY HOME
AVOID GATHERING
Oh, I remember! I was little, but I remember that my parents wouldn't let me to go the playground! Our school was closed too, and we weren't allowed to visit our relatives.
Not only schools! Everything was closed! People were told to stay home, roads were empty, and there was no air travel. Most countries were in lockdown. Since we survived, though, shouldn't we be grateful?

Ugh, let's change the topic.
That one is too scary.
Let me share somethingdifferent
Last week my mouth was very sore,
and I still can't chew very well.
Oh, really?
I'm lucky, I guess.
I have no problems chewing...

But
A couple of weeks ago,
I had an issue with my tongue. I had a
fever, and I couldn't taste properly.
Whatever I ate, it seemed disgusting.

Wow, really?
Don't you think it's cool
how our tongue can
identify so many tastes?

Oh, one time I also had a bad cold,
and it was hard to eat.
I had such pain in my throat.
It was disgusting too!

Yeah, I've had that, too,
But now I feel fine, and I can eat what I like.
Should I be grateful?

Hey, We're talking about eating difficulties, but isn't interesting that our food is so delicious? How did that happen?
Hmm, that's a good question. You know, we have an apple tree at home. It gives us lots of apples, and they're very yummy.

Cool! We have a big backyard, and my parents plant strawberries, watermelons, and so on. They're yummy too. You should come and try some!
That sounds great, and thank you for the invitation! One day I will come over!

I am sure you'll be happy to see all our plants! Sometimes I think about how they can grow so many fruit.
Oh, I also think about how such little plants can grow so much fruit. That is definitely a good question!

I know what you mean!
But now I'm thinking...
Let's say I have no fingers.
How am I gonna play?
You know, I just remembered!
Last week I had a pain in my right hand.
It hurt me when I was trying to play.
Oh, never mind!

You know, one day I saw someone without a hand.
Oh, no!
Why if I had no fingers?
Don't say something like that!

Aaahh!
Let's change the topic!
That's too scary.
Let's think about our legs,
So that we can walk,
run, play soccer, and so on
Yes, legs are so important.
I like playing soccer in the summer,
as well as biking and things like that.

Yeah! One of my friends lost his leg
in an accident.
He was a good soccer player too.

That's horrible!

Yeah.
But let's change back to a less depressing topic. I love to eat fast food. What about you?
Yes, I like it, too! But my dad said we shouldn't eat too much of it!

Not only that
My dad said it's harmful
to our bodies as well.

Oh, no!
I love it so much.
Although he's right. If I eat too
much of it, I'll have stomach pains.

Oh, yeah!
But it's not bad to eat it.
It's delicious.
Yes, it is.
I am not talking about
it being bad,
Just that too much
isn't good for you.

Oh, I see
That's true, we have to
eat a balanced diet.
A balanced diet?
What do you mean?

It just means a diet that helps us to be healthy and energetic. It helps make us strong and protects our bodies!
That is good information! But still, there is a possibility of being sick or having stomach pain!

Hmm, so what should we do?
Yes, I am thinking.....

We definitely have to take care of our bodies...
Yes, because if we get sick, we may have to take medicine or go see a doctor! That's what you mean, right?

Mmm, sort of.
But going to the doctor and taking medicine means that we care for ourselves.
Even so, though, shouldn't we be grateful to the doctor?
Yes, definitely, but actually, a lot of people help us every day.
And we should be grateful to them too.

Don't you ever wonder who controls the sickness, created the doctors, and gave the scientists the brains to invent and prepare the medicines?
Let's think about it this way. There is no doubt that we have to care for ourselves, but there is still the possibility of getting sick.

Sure, I have to wonder.
But what do you think?
Isn't there someone we should be grateful to all the time? Someone who keeps us healthy and makes us wise?
Yes, that is our Creator! All of these things come from our Creator and we should be grateful to our Creator for everything!

SOME OF OUR BELOVED BOOKS

1. I am searching! Wait a minute!
   We are searching too!
2. Are we grateful enough?
3. We may look different!
4. Greetings:
   what are they good for?
5. I love... positive affirmations
   for children

6. I don't care! Wait a moment!
   We care!
7. Work hard, dream big
8. Manners help
   the world go round!
9. Confidence means power
10. Learning is wonderful

INFO@KIDSEDUCARE.CA
ZABEDM@KIDSEDUCARE.CA

Copyright © 2022 by Zabed Mohammad,
All rights reserved
CANADA.
Library of Congress Cataloging-in-publication Data
ISBN: 978-1-7388326-2-0

Publisher: Kids Edu Care Inc.
Children's Dedicated Learning Series
Website: www.kidseducare.ca
Illustration Copyright © 2022 by
Kids Edu Care Inc.

Illustration & Design
Bee Digital